Philosophy of the Creative Process

In order to be creative, one must recognize the source of all creation, the Great Spirit. The Great Spirit created the universe, the stars, the moon, the galaxies, earth, people, animals, trees, plants, and so on. If the Great Spirit created everything, then it follows that the Spirit is in everything, in all of creation. I am not a religious person, but I am a spiritual person, because I, like you and all of creation, were created by the Great Spirit.

It is this spirit that unites us all into one global family. All of us live in relationship, to one another, to our environment, and to our spiritual creator. The Great Spirit is a positive spirit that produces positive energy, honesty, truth, enlightenment, and trust. However, there is a negative spirit active in the world that produces negative energy, deception, dishonesty, fear, power, and control.

My creative process I call illuminism because it attempts to use the positive energy of the Great Spirit to portray our unity of spirit and that element we have in common—the positive spiritual energy of all mankind.

There is so much in the world that divides us. Conflict is created when someone wants something and someone else doesn't want them to have it. We are divided by ideology, beliefs, opinions, nationality, and customs. We will never agree with one another on any issue, so the best we can do is to respectfully agree to disagree. However, we can be united in the Spirit, and that is my goal. We must learn to respect one another, value the beliefs and opinions of those with whom we disagree, and allow people the freedom of the Spirit. We must encourage free trade, free exchange of ideas, free movement of people, and freedom to govern ourselves. Winston Churchill once said, "Democracy is the worst possible form of government, but it beats anything else that has been tried from time to time."

Monopolies, dictatorships, anything where a few people control the spirit and destiny of the majority, does nothing but stifle the Spirit and goes against the intent of the Great Spirit. The one thing that separates us from the Great Spirit, is our ego. It has been said that sin is spelled with a capital "I," when me, myself and I become the most important thing in our life, then the Great Spirit retreats from us and the Spirit of Darkness enters. We become filled with the desire for self-satisfaction, and in order to achieve maximum satisfaction of self, we become dishonest, deceitful, untruthful, full of jealousy, envy, hate, and bitterness.

Freedom of the Spirit is what creates an environment for people to become creative, to maximize the creative genius that is within them, given by the Great Spirit. Governments and institutions should create an environment where people can be free to express their creative powers, however, most governments and institutions do just the opposite. They create an environment where the majority of the people are subject to the will and domination of a few. The few who are in the position of power and control, tend to wield that power and control over the heads of the majority like a hammer, trying to create subjects rather than equals.

However, the old structures are gradually changing. We are moving from an industrial society to an information society, an environment where people can have more control of their own destiny. An environment where unions, churches, and other institutions will have less

Illuminism

I believe that within each of us, there is a Spirit of Light and a Spirit of Darkness. The Spirit of Light manifests itself by unconditional love, truth, forgiveness and reconciliation. The Spirit of Darkness manifests itself by hatred, jealousy, revenge, anger and destruction. I believe it is the responsibility of every artist to reflect the Spirit of Light.

I believe that poetry should be the international language of the Spirit of Light. All art is spiritual, an outward expression of an inner spirit. I try to bring out the light in my poetry, to inspire, enlighten and uplift the spirit and thoughts of people around the world.

So much in our world today is driven by the Spirit of Darkness—art and humor that degrade people, rather than uplift and inspire. So much in our world is driven by money, power and control that the human spirit is compromised and many times crushed, so that people lose hope and resort to acts of violence.

I believe it is the responsibility of every leader, every artist and especially every poet to work to restore the Spirit of Light within people all over the world. People are hungry for food for their souls as well as their bodies. People need the Spirit of Light that gives them hope, renewal, motivation, and a new sense of direction.

As a poet, I feel inadequate to the task, but the Spirit of Light keeps encouraging me to write and share my inner vision with those who choose to read it. Many will scoff at it, I'm sure, but to those who read it and gain inspiration and enlightenment, that alone gives me motivation to continue.

power and control, and individuals will gain more control of the information that is available on the Internet and elsewhere, and have free use of their individual spiritual powers to create new and exciting ideas. The old phrase "Power to the people" is becoming a reality—not as a political movement, but as a natural evolution of the information age.

People should not be forced to join any institution in order to have employment and create a meaningful life for themselves, they should be free to dream their dreams and set goals for themselves as the Spirit leads them. Illuminism is about seeing the light and following the light as the Spirit of Light gives us direction. I am an independent thinker, I am not a follower of movements, right or left, and I dislike propaganda and egoists who think they are smart because they are rich, have advanced degrees, work for the government, work for a large corporation, or any other rationalization they may conjure up in their minds. Egoists are great in their own mind, but to others in the world, they are boring and self-centered.

If one wants to be great, then one must become a servant of all, must humble themselves, and put others first. One must be constantly aware of the Great Spirit and that the power of the Spirit is in every living thing, not just other people, but in the trees, the plants, the mountains, the streams, the glaciers, and all of creation. The Great Spirit created diversity and we have the power to create unity within that diversity, through respect and honor of one another with emphasis on the Spirit that is within us, for the Great Spirit will unite us.

SECTION I

A Spirit Sings

Respect	3	Acronyms	29
World Hunger	4	Truth	30
Common Sense	5	Lily of the Valley	31
The Goal	6	Kongsvinger	32
Life Support	7	The Golden Wedding	33
Olympic Spirit	8	USS Alaska	34
The Troll	9	USS Juneau	35
Ye Ol' Leprechaun	10	Peace Through Poetry	36
Sue	11	The Second Coming	37
Left and Right	12	Operation Moses	38
Russ	13	The Last Shall Be First	39
Churches	14	A World Beyond War	40
Crushing the Spirit	15	The Theatre	41
Inner Beauty	16	The Soldier	42
Segregation	17	Malpractice	43
The Lights	18	Money, Power and Control	44
Nimbus	19	Take Not Thy Spirit	45
Peace	20	The Great Spirit	46
The Oceanic Sense	21	Candle Power	47
Middlessence	22	Peacemakers	48
Summer Visitors	23	Peace Is Nonprofit	49
Expert	24	Young Eyes	50
Move	25	The Drum	51
Capital Punishment	26	Deception	52
Unity	27	Voice in the Wilderness	53
The Perfect Union	28		

Respect

Peace comes with respect—
    Respect for person,
    Respect for heritage,
    Respect for religion.

People need not agree to respect—
    Respect for family,
    Respect for age,
    Respect for knowledge.

Attitude is most important—
    Respect for nationality,
    Respect for minorities,
    Respect for gender.

Respect is the key to peace—
But it must be earned.

World Hunger

Hunger is a problem
In many parts of the earth.
Wars, famine, and flood
Are causes before birth.

Population has nearly doubled
Since 1965,
With 60 percent of humanity
Living within 60 miles of a sea coast.

Weather patterns are changing,
With carbon emissions on the rise.
Heavy industry in all countries
Contribute to the demise.

Hunger, nutrition, and water
Are problems for the many.
Those that have are satisfied
But are those without any?

Common Sense

Two cents were rolling along one day
    Speaking common sense by the bay,
Penny Cents and Minnie Cents
    Were speaking in their humble way.

Penny Cents said to Minnie Cents,
    "What is the sense of cents?
It makes no sense to have cents in a sense,
    We only confuse the dense."

Said Minnie Cents to Penny Cents
    "The money market smells like the fish market
The scents make no sense
    To us cents."

"To praise God in His Glory
    Makes more sense,
Than to honor the dense who sit on the fence,"
    Said Penny to Minnie Cents.

And so the cents rolled along
    Wondering if the dense would come to their sense
And make them feel the magnificence,
    Not like a couple of cents.

The Goal

Winning isn't everything—
It is how you play the game.
To enjoy the sport is more important
Than glory or fame.

Life is not about winning—
It is about enjoying the quest.
To enjoy the birds, flowers and stars
Makes it all the best.

To defeat another human
Is not my goal in life.
It is to enjoy his diversity
And to have empathy for his strife.

To enjoy life and nature
Is what my goal should be.
For it is not awards I'm after,
It is proving my worth to me.

Life Support

A friend was dying
In a hospital bed,
His life dependent
On a life support machine.

A cleaning lady
Came in one day,
Unplugged the life support
For her vacuum cleaner.

My friend died
While she cleaned the room,
He is dead
But the floor is clean.

Olympic Spirit

The Olympic flame
Burns on forever,
The Eternal flame
Burns in our hearts.

The inner Spirit
Drives us to excel,
To be what God
Created us to be.

No act of terrorism
Or natural disaster,
Can extinguish the flame
Because it is Spirit.

The inner Spirit
Will dwell forever,
The Great Spirit of God
Will live within us.

The Troll

I walked out on a little knoll,
looked across the valley
and saw to my surprise
an old Norwegian Troll.

With a nose as long
as his tail
and belly as round
as his head.

He said, "To myself
alone be enough."
Our country's mood
Is the same ol' stuff.

Ye Ol' Leprechaun

Me eyes were rather blurry
As I drank me green Irish beer,
The girls were gettin' prettier
The distant ones seemed near.

I blink me eyes once or twice
Dreamin' O' me Ireland,
Me thinks I'm in Dublin
Or by the sea and the sand.

I look down the bar to me left
And there to me surprise,
Is a Leprechaun a smilin'
With a sparkle in his eyes.

I says, "Welcome to the Galleon."
"Have ye tried the lamb Irish stew?"
He says, "I've tried it,
Now me wants a brew."

I says, "Where are the lassie Leprechauns?"
He says, "Oh, if I only knew."
Here we sits, two lonely lads
All we wants—is you.

Sue

When someone stares at you, sue.
When someone swears at you, sue.
When someone glares at you, sue.
When in doubt, sue.

Litigation is a part of life
But it has become ridiculous.
Everyone looking to sue everyone
And no one taking responsibility.

Lawyers win, people lose
Just as no one wins a strike.
Only those called to mediate
Arc paid a healthy fee.

Lawyers run for office
So they can pass laws,
To keep the system going
And to keep the money flowing—to them.

Left and Right

The right, self-righteous
In their minds they are always right.
If you disagree with them,
You are wrong.

The left, pseudo-intellectual
In their minds they are always correct.
If you disagree with them,
You are stupid.

Between the left and right
Is the independent thinker,
Despised by both camps
But able to think for themselves.

The right and left
Self-righteous and pseudo-intellectual,
Legends in their own minds
But full of B.S.

Russ

Much has been written about Vikings
Those who went to sea,
They explored, roared and gored
The ancestors of you and me.

Those that went inland
Much less is known,
Perhaps their stories were less romantic
But from them Nations have grown.

The inland Vikings
Were known as Russ,
They invaded, raided
And created such a fuss.

Russ were feared by many
And loved by some of the same,
But it is from these inland Vikings
That Russia got its name.

Churches

Churches are in the business
of religion,
Teaching theology as taught
in their seminaries.

Churches are in the business
of politics,
Trying to do the work
of bureaucrats.

Churches are in the business
of self-perpetuation,
Trying to keep their structure
and their clergy going.

Spirituality is dying
Poetry must keep it alive.

Crushing the Spirit

The government does it:
By making people dependent,
Putting them on reservations and in
ghettos.

The schools do it:
By regimentation and labeling,
separating students into those who can and can't.

The churches do it:
By defining how the Holy Spirit works,
So only the clergy can control the sacraments.

Business and labor do it:
By defining jobs and categorization of
people's talents and duties.

Families do it:
By put-downs and ridicule,
neglect and abuse.

But the spirit lives!

Inner Beauty

So much ado is made
about beauty in America.
Millions of dollars are spent
trying to look beautiful.

Beauty pageants, beauty salons,
beautiful people,
beautiful bodies—
Blah!

There is no greater beauty
in woman or man,
than the inner beauty
that radiates the soul.

The beauty of character—
honesty, compassion,
understanding, forgiveness, and tolerance
are all in short supply.

Segregation

Segregation in America
reaches its peak
on Sunday morning.

People segregate by
religion, race, culture
and nationality.

Nature lovers go for walks,
hike in the mountains,
or watch the rivers flow.

Skeptics and nonbelievers
read, write, or sleep
in their homes.

Man speaks through Science,
The Spirit speaks through poetry.

The Lights

When we lived in Seattle
Boeing laid off over 50,000 employees.
The mayor said,
"I'll turn out the lights."

When my mother and father
died in 1992,
I felt like
someone had turned out the lights.

Sometimes I feel like
turning out the lights,
but I know the eternal light
glows forever.

That inner light
provides the inspiration,
illumines the soul,
and beams out from time to time.

Nimbus

Oh Nimbus, oh Nimbus,
What art thou? Art thou art?
Thou must be, because if
thou art not, then what?

If beauty thou be,
then be it not to me.
If beauty be in the eye,
then my eye cannot see.

A symbol? Ah yes.
For what? The blues?
Perhaps more meaning with
various hues.

Some say blue with gold
for the flag nearby.
Some say yellow and orange
for the evening sky.

Some say white
for the winter to come.
I say red,
a big sore thumb!

Peace

Peace is a word
of many connotations,
spoken in churches
of all denominations.

For Humanism—
through the process of education,
it means perfection,
constant dedication.

For Communism—
it means one world culminated,
nations living in harmony
with dissidents eliminated.

For Christianity—
it means submission of
the ego to Christ—
a higher commission.

Will there be peace?
What will it be?
Think of how to achieve it,
and what kind for you and me.

The Oceanic Sense

Waves,
winds,
wash with seas,
wide . . .
far . . .
deep.

Powers,
saves,
devours . . .
graves . . .
sleeps.

Smooth sands wash,
worlds waste away . . .
Petros stands!

Why?
Where?
Which?

        David Moe

Middlessense

Searching, searching for meaning . . .
Where, oh where, can it be?
Fulfillment and satisfaction
is what life ought to be, for me.

Searching, searching for meaning . . .
Is that it? Over there?
Perhaps a Ph.D.,
or a simple love affair.

Search, searching for meaning . . .
Does that come with middle age?
Maybe I'll climb a mountain
or contemplate with a sage.

Searching, searching for meaning . . .
What is it I have said?
Shall I become an astronomer?
I think I'll go to bed.

Summer Visitors

Rivers flow,
glaciers moan with labor pain,
giving birth to Spring
again.

People visit . . . ah,
politicians, too . . .
then go home
to tell us what to do.

Sometimes they stay
for a whole week
to do a thorough study
of the meek.

Why don't they come in Winter
to feel the ice?
Only in Summer
when things are nice.

Expert

The world is full of experts,
consultants and all of that;
people who were totally ignored
when the world was flat.

Now there is so much to know,
one can't comprehend it all,
so we listen to experts
who specialize in falderal.

One expert will tell you black is white,
another that white is black,
but when it comes to a decision,
you're on your own, Jack.

What is an expert, anyway?
That I do not know.
But if he has a briefcase,
chances are he'll tell you so.

Move

When my daughter was small,
she toddled to the kitchen wall,
and simply said,
"Move."

With the Winter comes the snow
and politicians to Juneau.
The message each year
is clear:
"Move."

When I'm secure within my grave,
I pray my wife will join nearby
when it is time for her to die,
but I hope her spirit does not cry,
"Move."

Capital Punishment

Is it right to kill a man
before his time?
Is it right to kill a city
before its prime?

Does not the life of a man
belong to his Creator?
Are not the foundations of a city
more than its theatre?

To punish a man by taking his life,
to punish a city through dissolution and strife
are destructive forces created by greed,
forces that Alaska doesn't need.

Capital punishment is the
flip of a switch;
capital punishment is a
Mat-Su pitch.

Unity

Who owns the mountains?
Who owns the trees?
Will he who owns them,
step forward, please?

Who owns the land?
Who owns the seas?
Will he who owns them,
step forward, please?

Who owns the world?
Who owns the space?
Will he who owns them,
take his honored place?

Who will bring us together,
unite us all?
For united we stand,
divided we fall.

Men have failed before,
they will do it again,
the Holy Spirit unites,
all else is a *sham!*

The Perfect Union

He said, "I'm only a carpenter,
but will you marry me?"
She said, "I'm only a maiden
with a baby."

He said, "We have not slept together,
how can this be?"
She said, "The Holy Spirit
did this for me."

He said, "The Holy Spirit!
What shall I tell my peers?"
She said, "Believe me,
for I have had only tears."

He said, "Any son of yours
is good enough for me."
She said, "He'll be your son, too.
Together we'll be three."

Acronyms

Language is a curious art
for those who are and are not so smart.
If you want to communicate,
use an acronym for bait.
Politics are not for everyone;
only those who do want fun
with DEM, GOP, JFK,
triple H, d-2, and peanut-one.
Government itself can be nice
with bureaucrats being most precise
with CIA, WHO, BIA,
AG, SOB, CG, and ICE.
Business also plays the game,
impressing people with the same—
BG, PYA, RE, B of A,
M&M, MGM, and AIM.
Oh, if we could procreate
like we communicate,
who would know his child
or dare ask his name?

Truth

What is truth?
A question for generations
asked by youths and sages
through ages of imagination.

Philosophers, politicians,
doctors, and musicians,
students and explorers,
witches and magicians.

Truth is not an idea,
philosophy or position;
truth is not a concept,
it defies definition.

Truth is a person—
Jesus Christ to be exact:
"I am the Way, the Truth, the Life,"
This I take as fact.

Truth is a person?
How can this be?
Get to know *Him,*
then you will see.

Lily of the Valley
May 5, 1985

Song of Solomon 2:2

*The bridegroom and the bride,
standing side by side . . .
The lily of the valley,
The lily among the thorns.*

*The bride loves the groom,
the groom loves the bride . . .
A union of believers
standing side by side.*

*Shepherd of the Valley
is the lily of the valley,
as the lily among thorns,
so is my love in the valley.*

Kongsvinger

A Norwegian church in the
middle of a field
built by twenty-eight Norwegians and one Swede—
the root of my being,
the rock that I need.

Visiting the church left memories
of picnics, laughter, and fun,
of people, gone now . . . most everyone.

The barn still stands,
the hitching post, too.
The firecrackers, the races, the cigar smoke . . .
I suppose they don't mean much to you.

To me they are memories
of days gone by.
Oh, each day is precious . . .
Don't make a soul cry.

The Golden Wedding
August 1931–1981

Two young people swear a solemn pact,
How do opposites attract?
Begun during depression years,
with dreams replacing all those fears.

Children are born,
neighbor boys die . . .
The big war made many cry.

Life goes on,
children grow . . .
Dentists, doctors, and college
are where the dollars go.

What keeps people together
for fifty years
in an era when people
are changing gears?

Is it sharing, trust,
accepting the dove?
It's all of that, plus,
Faith, Hope, and Love!

USS Alaska

Another boat
built to destroy,
manned by men,
no longer boys.

A boat to go
under the sea,
built to protect
you and me.

Some will protest,
some will complain,
but when the threat is real,
they will refrain.

A boat of steel,
no longer of wood,
be not overcome by evil,
but overcome evil with good.

USS JUNEAU
November 13, 1942

The battle of Guadalcanal,
the JUNEAU hit by a torpedo.
Then another . . .
she was sinking fast.

The five Sullivan brothers
all went to their grave,
plus three Combs,
two Rogers . . .
brave.

One hundred and fifty, blown to the blue.
Their red blood
with the white foam . . .
Ten left in the crew.

The USS JUNEAU
remembered this day,
seven hundred down to sea . . .
gone for eternity.

Peace Through Poetry

Peace on earth,
the angels sing.
Good will to men,
for it is Spring.

The Prince of Peace
had come to earth,
to bring God's love
from His very birth.

Peace, Brotherhood, and Love,
from the lips of angels,
from the wings
of a dove

Poets can say it,
priests can pray it,
singers can sing it,
but *we must live it.*

The Second Coming

Twenty centuries of waiting
for Christ to return . . .
The cradle has been rocking
when will the earth burn?

The devil has been loosed,
anarchy is in the air.
The Antichrist will rule supreme
until Christ is here.

We live in luxury and self-indulgence,
fat with food and drink,
while much of the world starves.
Oh, what does Jesus think?

The world is falling apart,
leaders cannot lead.
The forces of evil control
Warning signs we do not heed.

Wait a little longer—
then as a thief in the night
Jesus Christ will return
to take his own aright.

Operation Moses

The four horsemen
came riding across the land—
famine rode through
Ethiopia.

The Jewish people
raised 460 million
to bring the Falasha Jews
to Israel.

Thousands of years ago,
Moses said, *"Let my people go."*
But in 1985,
Colonel Mariam said, *"No!"*

With three billion in armaments,
Ethiopia, Libya and Iran
unite in their hatred
of Israel.

The Last Shall Be First

Faith is belief in the invisible—
to believe what we cannot see.
God helps us to understand
the opposite of what appears to be.

To bring us life, He puts our "self" to death.
To make us saintly, He makes us sinners.
To raise us up, He casts us down . . .
His justice is revealed through injustice.

He who would be most, must become least,
to serve, rather than *be* served.
The first shall be *last,*
and the last shall be *first.*

Where understanding falters,
Faith dances . . .
When life ends,
immortality begins.

A World Beyond War

The old world
has known many wars.
Men have separated themselves,
closed all the doors.

Civil wars, gang wars,
thirty-year wars,
holy wars, race wars,
and the war
to end all wars.

No weapon has ever been created
that hasn't been used in war . . .
gas, bacteria,
booby traps and knives,
every imaginable device
to destroy human lives.

Let us imagine
a world beyond war,
where people are tolerant of others,
and there is fighting no more.

The Theatre

Before my wife and I
were married,
I told her of my true love—
the theatre.

Many years have past,
our children have grown.
I love my wife more now,
but my old love beckons home.

The lights, the makeup,
the costumes and the glare,
but it's the actors
for whom I really care.

The seeds were planted early.
The stage is home to me,
to sing and dance and laugh,
or just to go and see.

We grow older,
the choices are always there.
God and family will be first—
the theatre I will share.

The Soldier
(a pawn of someone's ego)

To go
or desert . . .
The choice is yours
for all eternity.

To train
or go AWOL . . .
The choice is yours
for all eternity.

Advance and be shot
or retreat and be shot . . .
The choice is yours
for all eternity.

Kill and be condemned
or return and be condemned . . .
The choice is yours
for all eternity.

Live with guilt
or live with shame . . .
The choice is yours
for all eternity.

Hell on earth
or Hell forever . . .
The choice is yours
for all eternity.

Malpractice

Doctors and lawyers are at war
  Over the cost of malpractice.
Each blames the other
  For their practice.

Insurance premiums are high
  Due to jury awards and investments.
Everyone is out for
  Profit.

The patient is left
  To fend for themselves.
Maybe some hclp
  And maybe not.

Self-interest is the bottom line,
  Doing what is best for me.
If people die in the process
  Let it be—let it be.

Money, Power, and Control

Money gives power
   To those who hunger for control.
Money, power, and control
   Is more important than soul.

What does it profit a man
   To gain the world and lose his soul?
Soul is not important
   To those who want control.

Who can control the soul?
   Certainly not those who seek
Money and Power,
   For the soul is spirit.

The spirit will live on
   When power and control are gone.
You can't take it when you go,
   So why be concerned with control?

Take Not Thy Spirit

We are lonely men,
   Quiet men,
Men who never say
   "Amen."

We live in the bowels
   of a ship,
We are starving to death.
   The Spirit has left us.

We pour urine over our heads,
   We watch our bodies wither.
We drink the bilge water,
   The stench of death is here.

Take not thy Spirit from us
   Oh Lord,
Take not thy Spirit
   From us.

The Great Spirit

The Great Spirit created
    All things—visible and invisible.
The Great Spirit
    Is in all things.

"Even the stones cry out
    For justice,"
The trees, mountains, glaciers,
    Bears, goats and sheep.

The Great Spirit is in all,
    All are brothers and sisters.
We need to respect one another
    And honor the Great Spirit.

The Great Spirit created each
    According to their understanding,
Do not quarrel about religion—
    The Great Spirit knows what is best.

Candle Power

Within each of us
    There is a flicker of light.
A candle is burning,
    Illuminating our soul.

This illumination of hope
    Is the Spirit within us,
Burning to be free,
    Not to be snuffed out.

The Great Spirit
    Gives each of us this light
And motivation to go on
    In spite of it all.

So many forces want to put it out
    But it burns eternally.
Candle power—power of the people
    To survive and prosper.

Peacemakers
October 1986

Anchorage Airport at 6:50 a.m.
      ready to leave for L.A.,
the first leg of a journey
      to bring goodwill from Toksook Bay.

Alaska Performing Artists for Peace
      proclaim a statement to the world
that citizens can make a difference
      while diplomats are bored.

Common people who want peace,
      willing to share their joys
in songs and dance
      with their girls and boys.

Peace is the goal?
      Isn't that rather odd?
Jesus said, *"Blessed are the peacemakers*
      for they shall be called the children of God."

Peace Is Nonprofit

Peace is nonprofit,
and therefore not popular.
Perpetual progress
is.

Power for peace,
power is the program.
Perpetual power
is popular.

Profit is the motive,
greed is the need.
Green is the color
to preach power.

Few get wealthy.
Many die
for the benefit
of the few.

No money for peace,
only for arms.
Arms create jobs,
jobs create votes.

Young Eyes

Young eyes that look at us,
watching every move,
looking to see what we do,
looking and watching.

Young eyes that say,
"Do not destroy my beauty,
do not destroy my future,
do not destroy my pleasant dreams."

Young eyes that watch
our generation of
violence, drugs, and vice,
going for the gusto,
regardless of the price.

Young eyes that observe,
question, and obey,
in order to write our history
someday.

The Drum

The drum
is a symbol of peace . . .
When there is conflict
beat the drum.

We dance, we sing
to each other,
to the rhythm
of the drum.

Drum . . . drum,
drum, drum, drum;
dance, sing, love
to the rhythm
of the drum.

Deception

We live in a country
where politicians program computers,
so their favorite candidate
can win the election.

We live in a country
where drugs are pushed to employees
by top management
down to the plants.

We live in a country
where the president
uses operatives to circumvent
the will of Congress.

We live in a country
where ministers of the gospel
fight verbal warfare on television
for ownership of a scam operation.

We live in a country
that has lost its ideals,
lost its sense of values
and we expect our young people to die for it.

Voice in the Wilderness

There is a voice in the wilderness . . .
Do you hear it?
It is speaking to you—
Listen . . .

Listen to years of experience,
frustration, mistakes,
child-rearing, house payments,
bad breaks.

Listen to learn
listen for fun
listen for any reason—
my time is soon done.

If you can learn from my errors
progress will be made—
I'll have been paid.

SECTION II

Portrait Poems

Old Adam	57	The Mayor	73
Cynthia Faulkins	58	The Twins	74
Mrs. Ben Smith	59	Lincoln of Alaska	75
Ed Dohrn	60	Fisherpersons	77
Lonewolf Smith	61	Grammar Anderson	79
Mr. Roberts	62	Uncle John	80
Oscar	63	Mel	81
Carol Beery Davis	64	Ruth	82
Amos Berg	65	Saint John	83
Dr. Rude	66	Saint Jamie	84
Montana Bill	67	E. Z. Smith	85
Tiger Olson	68	Allen Yee	86
Blue Belle	69	The Fish Pirate	87
Simeon	70	J.F.K. Remembered	88
Jesus	71	Carol	89
The Mailman	72		

Old Adam

Adam was the first of all,
not too fat and not too tall.
Then Eve came along
And made that man awfully small.

Eve was the first of women—
she came on with a flare.
But when it came time to dine,
she had nothing to wear.

Adam fell from grace,
as did she.
We have been living with this,
for many a century.

We are by nature
sinful and unclean—
the nature of Adam
is everywhere to be seen.

Adam is in me,
no matter what I do.
He keeps coming back,
as Eve comes back to you.

Cynthia Faulkins

An elderly lady,
When I was a boy.
She was the town gossip,
Gathering news was a joy.

In her backyard
She had a well—
The town gathering spot—
And stories to tell.

Everyone knew
Everyone's business,
Even the cats and dogs
Were accounted for.

Cynthia left a
Strange smell in the air.
When she left the house,
We would smell her chair.

She wrote a weekly article
For the *Daily Night.*
She was paid by the column inch,
So the news was long, but trite.

I shall never forget
This woman,
This woman who gathered the news
When there was none.

Mrs. Ben Smith

The raunchiest woman
I ever knew,
She swore, cussed,
Even chewed.

No one knew her first name
And no one ever asked.
She was the grandmother
Of my friend.

Playing in the yard
One hot summer day,
She sat on the steps
While we were busy at play.

A neighbor man came to visit.
She lifted her skirt,
Then she spread her legs
Giving us a beaver shot.

It was at that moment
I decided not to become a doctor.
Mrs. Ben Smith,
Where are you now?

Ed Dohrn

The first volunteer from
Alaska in World War I,
is what he claimed
to everyone.

Upon his return after the war
he had been promised
a homestead,
but it was no more.

Soon after his retirement,
his money was gone,
a few days in the hospital
and a life's savings withdrawn.

At a visit shortly before he died,
he showed me a picture
of his battalion with pride.
"What is that cement slab?" I'd chide.
"Oh, that's where Lt. MacArthur
gave his V.D. lectures," he replied.

Lonewolf Smith

There was a man
from Meyers Chuck
with good vocabulary,
but bad luck.

He was a loner
with a pen for a friend,
letters to the editor
to see his name again.

His pen name
was *Lonewolf Smith,*
his letters
were mostly myth.

One day they stopped
as did he . . .
my loss—
not making the effort to see.

Mr. Roberts

Who was Mr. Roberts?
Did he have a first name?
Henry Fonda played the part well
on stage and on the screen.

Every ship has a Mr. Roberts
a man the others respect.
Mr. Roberts doesn't come with rank
but with character.

The Mr. Roberts I knew
provided comfort during a mess.
The Mr. Roberts I knew
was called simply Jess.

Oscar

My father's name was Oscar
My mother used to say.
"I got my Oscar
in 1931."

The Academy Awards
give out their Oscar,
to the best artists
in the motion picture industry.

Where does the name originate?
From King Oscar?
Oscar Meyer or
is it derived from Oskar?

Oscar is a household word
to millions of people,
Oscar is a special name
for me.

Carol Beery Davis

She called me a poet
before I had written a poem.
She called me a musician
before I had sung a song.

This woman of Alaska,
Mother of Alaska,
With her love of music, literature,
and all that is fine.

She has gone to
the land of rest,
Poet Laureate of Alaska
what cross is yours?

Amos Berg

I salute you
Amos Berg,
man of the sea
and river runner.

You explored
the Yukon, Snake,
Columbia, Missouri, Mississippi,
and many more.

You are right.
We need to get back to nature,
to the real world of rivers,
rapids, and rain.

Our lives are based on
images,
images on TV, movies,
and videos.

Amos Berg, I salute you.

Dr. Rude

A medic during
World War One—
then to medical school
to help someone.

Came to Alaska
in the 1920s—
Ketchikan, Petersburg, Juneau,
not just for the monies.

He was a friend
singing in the choir—
cutting wood, going fishing,
never a liar.

He cared by Amy
until her dying day—
feeding her, combing her hair,
it was his way.

We go through life
only one time—
but a friend like Dr. Rude,
is more rare than a gold dime.

Montana Bill

In a small house on a large lot
near Montana Creek
resides an old-timer . . .
alone.

Russian immigrant, gold miner,
with a hard body and soft heart,
few friends, but many memories . . .
forgotten.

Took him a King Salmon one day,
he told me to pick his fresh strawberries
For my family . . .
kind.

The Winter snow came—
silent in his bed,
sidewalks not shoveled . . .
dead.

Tiger Olson

Growl like a tiger
even if you can't,
an old man
is free to chant.

An old man
in a pioneer home,
after years in Taku Inlet—
a spirit free, alone.

A real tiger
in a prior life?
Who will dispute it?
Certainly not a wife!

He was gentle as a lamb,
ask any child . . .
How then a tiger?
A man so mild?

Blue Belle

Why are you blue?
Blue Belle
Why are your thoughts like glue?
Blue Belle.

Blue are your eyes
as blue as the skies,
Blue are your stockings
to cover the black and blue markings.

Why are you lesbian?
Do you prefer women
because the men in your life
have been abusive and brutal?

Come to me,
Blue Belle,
I will not hurt you.
You will never be blue again.

Simeon

Simeon was old,
about to die,
but he had a dream
to see the babe.

When the child was brought,
he took him in his hands.
He looked at the child
and saw hope for all lands.

He said, *"Now let thy servant
depart in peace,
for mine eyes have seen
thy salvation."*

Simeon was at peace,
ready to depart,
not afraid of sin or death
but with comfort in his heart.

Jesus

Son of God
and son of man
came not to condemn,
but to redeem.

He preached repentance,
confession,
and forgiveness
of sins.

Jesus chose laymen
to carry the good news.
He was born into a barefoot world
and cricified by those with shoes.

 David Moe

The Mailman

There was a man
who lived far from Tok
and walked miles for his mail,
it was no joke.

A new mailman came one day
citing postal regulations,
telling he had to have a box
or no mail.

The man said, *"Give me my mail."*
The postman said, *"No."*
"Then tomorrow I bring a rifle."
Postman said, *"Ho, Ho!"*

The next day the man came
with his rifle to get his mail.
Postman cited more regulations
and died like a quail.

The man wanted his mail,
not regulations and B.S.
Washington was too far away
for all of this.

The Mayor

Chicken, Alaska in 1982
had an election, nothing new.
The issues of subsistence and abortion
were only a few.

A local publisher, Elmo Strumpet
by name,
offered a Thanksgiving turkey
to those who voted and came.

When the ballots were counted,
even though they were few,
Lo, Thanksgiving turkey became
Mayor, and Governor, too.

The "also ran" candidates,
the very next day,
ate His Honor for dinner,
to the voter's dismay.

Chicken voted for a turkey,
this story is true,
but then, other turkeys have won,
and were eaten alive, too.

David Moe

The Twins

One was physical,
the other spiritual;
one was hairy,
the other fair.

Esau was the eldest,
but Jacob got the birthright
for a mother's cunning
and a meal.

Rebekah had her favorite—
Jacob got the blessing,
Esau received . . .
only a meal.

Spiritual needs
are deep and real,
physical needs . . .
the next meal.

Lincoln of Alaska
(Frank Peratrovich)

Young Indian boy sent to Seattle,
with little sister in hand,
to meet an uncle on the bottle
who never showed.

Became a ward of the state,
went through Indian schools
and finally to Oregon
to an Indian high school.

Football was his game,
with a coach that played at Carlisle.
He had high expectations of Frank
all the while.

In his senior year
his coach took him to Portland
to meet an old friend—
Jim Thorpe.

Thorpe said, *"Go to college son,
you can always play football."*
So to college Frank did go,
playing football and continuing to grow.

Back to Alaska,
opened a store,
got married, grew in spirit
more and more.

Friends wanted Frank
in the legislature,
they wanted their children
in public schools
and laws to make them equal—
not to look like fools.

Frank served in Juneau,
had a distinguished career,
no longer had to sit in the balcony,
and could drink his beer.

Frank prepared the way
for generations to come.
Natives can hold their heads high,
Frank's job has been done.

Frank has gone,
responding to Lincoln's call . . .
Two men who believed in
human dignity for all.

Fisherpersons

Halibut Harry and Salmon Sal
went fishin'—many stories to tell
about the one that got away
and all of that.

Asked Salmon Sal of Halibut Harry,
"How many fish will this boat carry?
'Cause I've got a feelin'
it's gonna sink."

Said Halibut Harry to Salmon Sal,
"This boat'll carry more fish
than the devil can fry in Hell."

They baited their hooks
and let out the line,
draggin' herring
through the salty brine.

Then, the stories began to flow
'bout the times long, long ago,
when the fish jumped in the boat
and all of that.

Asked Salmon Sal of Halibut Harry,
"What's the biggest fish you
ever did carry?
'Cause I've got a feelin'
mine is bigger, still."

Said Halibut Harry to Salmon Sal,
"The biggest fish, no one could tell
'cause they had nothin'
to compare it with!"

"If you catch a fish
as big as that,
then they'll have somethin'
to measure at."

Asked Salmon Sal of Halibut Harry
"What are scales for,
if not to weigh fish
such as that?"

Said Halibut Harry to Salmon Sal,
"There is no scale
for fish or whale
when they reach the size
of all of that."

So it went all day long
with dialogue
soundin' like a song,
with no one really ever bein' wrong.

But the best story
that's ever been told,
is 'bout the one that got away
and all of that.

Grammar Anderson

An elderly lady trying to teach
Had lost her hearing, eyesight, and touch
Trying to teach an immature group
With some sensitivity, but not much.

A lady with a world of experience
Willing to share with all,
But we were unwilling to receive
It was our loss—her call.

She had known Mamie and Ike
When her husband was an Army Chaplain.
She had a sense of History
Literature, Culture, and Art.

She had so much to offer
But we saw only weakness and age (not nice).
We took advantage of her
Now we pay the price.

Uncle John

Music was in the air
Early morning to late at night.
Uncle John gave private lessons
In band, Chorus, and Orchestra all right.

Few teachers in America
Give their all
To a profession taken for granted,
Economic rewards that are small.

Uncle John was not there
For money or luxury abound.
He loved the music,
The students, and the sound.

Uncle John was an inspiration,
Especially to those who played slowly.
We admired the man
Known as Uncle John Solie.

Mel

Mel was the town cop
With badge and gun and uncouth,
But he was a man
Who understood youth.

Many times he chased us
Down the highway,
Only to turn around
To let us go—our way.

The carbon from the exhaust
Came out like black plumes,
His old Plymouth at 50 mph
Was covered with fumes.

Mel never turned us in
Or even took our license number.
He was the best cop
Any youth could remember.

Ruth
(Ruth 1:16)

Ruth was a widow
with a mother-in-law for a friend.
Naomi wanted her to return
to her own people again.

Ruth said, "Intreat me not to leave thee
or to return from following thee,
for whither thou goest, I will go;
and where thou lodgest, I will lodge;
thy people shall be my people,
and thy God my God."

Ruth found a new life,
new husband and new faith;
a wandering woman, lost and alone,
great-grandmother of David.

God uses what He wills
any way He can,
God uses me
and you, Ruth Ann.

Saint John

Upon arrival in Leningrad—
St. Peter was its original name—
we learned of Peter the Great,
St. Peter, St. Peter, and St. Peter.

We visited the museums—
St. Peter's Square, St. Peter's Fount,
St. Peter's Palace, St. Peter's Cathedral—
until we were petered out.

But on our journey through St. Peterdom,
we were privileged to be
accompanied by none other
than St. John.

St. John, whose voice had disappeared,
honored us with his presence,
even came to a few of the concerts
to hear what he had feared.

"There are no professional musicians
in our group," Dixie had said.
Oh, all those years of study for naught—
St. John had gone to bed.

  David Moe

Saint Jamie

There was a lady in Moscow
who had her eye on Jamie,
wanted an American husband.
There were no if's, and's, or maybe's.

Jamie said, "I'm too old for you,
you need a younger man."
She said, "I have four children already,
I think you will understand."

She said, "I'll be the best deal
you have ever had.
I need a rich American husband!"
Oh, it was all so very said.

That evening she confronted him again.
"Would you like to make love?" she asked.
"I'm going to bed to sleep," he said,
"What other use is there for a bed?"

Ah, Sainthood, is it worth all of this?
To trade a night of pleasure
for some unknown
heavenly bliss?

Some say, "Yes," some say, "No,"
some say, "Oh well."
I'll never know, or if I did,
I'd never tell.

E. Z. Smith

E. Z. Smith
was a client of mine;
he purchased life insurance
for $100 on a dime.

His wife wasn't E. Z.,
she was a Sitka belle;
she never purchased anything,
and I never tried to sell.

E. Z. wasn't easy,
but he did finally buy;
now he'll have some money
when it's time to die.

Writing poetry isn't easy,
but it's something for the many;
if you don't buy life insurance,
you deserve to die
without any.

Allen Yee

Today, Allen Yee
    Came to see me.
After 30 years
    Memories remain.

Yee—he was one
    Of the good guys
Working in a sea
    Of incompetence.

He has maintained
    His sanity
After all these years
Of inhumanity.

Yee, you see,
    Was smarter by degree
Than most of those who
    Could only disagree.

The Fish Pirate

My father-in-law
was a fish pirate;
my wife was the
fish pirate's daughter.

Rikard did the fishing,
so he could send
his little girl to college
in Iowa.

The fish pirate's daughter
returned to Ketchikan
to meet a school teacher
and get married.

Now I'm related
to half of Southeast Alaska,
I'm married to the land,
the sea, and the fish.

To think that all of this
began with one stubborn
Norwegian fisherman—
the fish pirate.

J.F.K. Remembered
November 22, 1963

A senior in college
on that tragic day,
hopes of the future shattered—
we could only pray.

The New Frontier
became the Last Frontier.
Idealism replaced with realism—
nothing held dear.

Then came Vietnam,
the mafia lurks.
The nation moved to pragmatism—
anything that works.

The nation has been in decline,
morals have been ignored.
We have no direction—
people are bored.

All that had been
is gone now.
I mourn for the youth
of tomorrow.

Carol

A beautiful mind
A sensitive soul
A fragile flower
A memory.

Quiet
Reflective
She maintained her sense of humor
Through it all.

Non-judgmental
Ready to forgive
Not wanting to burden others
With her problems.

The youngest of all
Yet the first to go.
Prepared, with faith,
That all is well.

SECTION III

Songs of the Soul

Song of the Soul	93		Time Out	125
Southern Women	94		Professional Pastors	126
Moe's Art	95		World Orchestra	127
The Sandwich Generation	96		Dog Gone	128
Ozone	97		The Erl King	129
Causes	98		Healing	130
Baptism	99		Theology	131
Desert Storm	100		U.S. Navy Memorial	132
Mother Earth	101		Control	133
Daughters of the Earth	102		The Body	134
Sunset	103		There Are Looks	135
Rhythm	104		God's Poems	138
The Key	105		The Garden	139
Biotechnology	106		Family Reunion	140
The Renaissance	107		Heavenly Host	141
Free Market	108		The Restless Soul	142
Nationalism	109		Prison	143
Pacific Rim League	110		Two Worlds	144
Women of 2000	111		Persons of Color	145
Religious Revival	112		The Office	146
Independence	113		Heartstrings	147
Mind Pollution	114		Poetry	148
Logic	115		Eye of Alaska	149
The Creation	116		Else	150
The Child	117		Pronouns	151
Inner Peace	118		Repression	152
Health Care Reform	119		Eat My Words	153
Rain	120		Rights	154
Cycle	121		Sports	155
Perseverance	122		Humor	156
Things	123		Nostradamus	157
Be Kind	124		Silence	158

Song of the Soul

I sing a love song
to the world,
to the world that suffers
prejudice, hate, and war.

I sing a love song
to the world,
to the world that suffers
AIDS, drug, and alcohol addiction.

I sing a love song
to the world,
to the world that suffers
domestic violence, child and sexual abuse.

I sing a love song
to the world,
to the world that suffers
pornography, pollution, and propaganda.

I sing a love song
to the world,
Oh, come, sing a love song
with me.

Southern Women

I like Southern women,
They like men.
They walk with grace,
They attract us men.

They still wear perfume,
Dresses, silk stockings and a smile.
They treat a man like a man
Keeping their dignity all the while.

Women who dislike men
grow cold and hard.
They talk only with other women
and try to act like men.

I don't care what they wear
or what they say,
It is their attitude.
They want domination and power.

Southern women,
don't lose it—
femininity is a precious gift.
God gives it—don't throw it away.

Moe's Art

When I listen to the music of
Mozart, Bach, Brahms,
Beethoven, or Wagner,
I know how insignificant is my art.

When I read the plays of
Sophocles, Goethe, Ibsen,
Shakespeare, or Brecht,
I know how insignificant is my art.

When I read the poems of
Milton, Keats, Yeats,
Dickinson, or Frost,
I know how insignificant is my art.

When I look at the
mountains, glaciers, rivers,
oceans, or streams,
The Spirit says, "God loves you too."

The Sandwich Generation

We are the sandwich generation
caring for our parents,
Our children, and grandchildren.
When will it end?

When the parent becomes
the child of the child,
roles are reversed—
our care should be mild.

Then we have the
needs of the spouse,
This takes our time and care.
Their needs are always there.

The children need our time,
Our love and concern.
They think they know it all
but have much to learn.

The grandchildren are also there
needing our love.
They are the joy of our life,
a gift from above.

All of these generations
need our special attention,
but our time is limited
for the sandwich generation.

Ozone

There is another issue
That is hitting home.
It is the issue
Of the ozone.

Chlorine, fluorine, and carbon,
Chlorofluorocarbons or CFC's
are what's causing
lung disease.

Man-made pollutants,
Air conditioners, aerosols,
and automobile exhaust—
Things that all of us need
at any cost.

The greenhouse effect, smog—
Where will it end?
Maybe not with a whimper
But with a gasp.

Causes

What is the cause
of the earth's demise?
Is it our fault
or the other guys?

Can it be
colonialism, imperialism,
socialism, communism,
capitalism, militarism,
or racism?

Maybe it is
sexism, consumerism,
nationalism, elitism,
or cannibalism?

I wonder what
happened to
individual responsibility?

Baptism
(October 1938)

The water flows over my head,
through my heart,
Through my being,
cleansing my soul.

Clear, fresh water
trickling from an eternal spring.
Clean, cleansing, cool,
caressing my body and soul.

Spiritual water
flows from the rock,
freeing my heart
for all eternity.

My baptism is complete—
I am a child of God.

Desert Storm
(February 23, 1991)

The ground war has begun.
Young lives will be lost
fighting a battle not their own,
a battle of will at any cost.

A dictator, Saddam Hussein,
ready to challenge the world
in a battle he cannot win,
but God is on his side.

God in His mercy
looks upon us
and shakes His head.
"I have no favorites," He said.

"All humans are my children,
I love all.
When will you understand my message?
I sent Moses, Isaiah, and Paul."

God loves us all,
not Jew more than Greek.
It seems so simple,
What more can I speak?

Mother Earth

The earth nourishes us
provides food, air, and water.
We must respect the earth
as our own mother.

Our father above watches
how we treat our mother.
if we do not treat her kindly,
our day is near.

We come to our mother
for strength and guidance.
The mountains, like breasts,
sustain us.

We must love our mother
for all she has given,
care for her
as she has cared for us.

Daughters of the Earth

Trees are the
Daughters of the earth,
Trees are our
Sisters.

Do not trim the trees
Or alter their style.
They know the forest,
They know us.

Do not tease
The trees—
You may contact
A tree disease.

Sunset
(In memory of my mother and father)

As the sun sets in Alaska,
the sun rises in Europe.
As the sun sets in Africa,
the sun rises in Siberia.

As a word goes out
from my land,
that word is received
in your land.

When the voices here
mourn the loss of a loved one,
the voices there
rejoice and welcome that one home.

Rhythm

Sometimes I think of rhythm
while writing poetry,
but I do not use
the rhythm method.

I think of the rhythm
of a flock of geese,
flying in formation
to their winter home.

I think of the rhythm
of Michael Jordan,
driving towards the basket
for another score.

I think of the rhythm
of a high diver,
as he twists and turns
before hitting the water.

I think of the rhythm
of nature,
whales swimming from Glacier Bay
to Hawaii and back again.

The Key

Everyone is looking for the key—
The key to your heart,
The key to success,
The key to salvation.

Everyone is born with a key—
a natural key.
Some people sing in the key of G,
others naturally in the key of D.

All of nature has a key—
the flowers bloom in A or E.
The rivers flow
to the C.

Some people think
in the key of F—
As for me,
I'm usually B.

Biotechnology

The age of Biology
is upon us.
Biotechnology is here to stay,
changing our DNA.

Genetic engineering will conquer
crop disease—
or so they say—
but changing our DNA?

When does life begin?
At conception or at delivery?
An important question in our day,
for they can change our DNA.

As one chromosome said to another,
"Turn around while I change my genes."
Changing my genes is OK,
but please, don't change my DNA.

The Renaissance

Are we moving into a new era
of the Renaissance of the arts?
Will poets become as popular
as football players?

Will the emphasis change
from baseball to ballet?
Will corporations invest more in the arts
than they do in sports?

Will people get tired
of the TV?
And turn to the higher forms
of opera and theatre?

Perhaps I will live in a new era,
a Renaissance of the arts,
Where an artist can make a living
like a computer operator.

 David Moe

Free Market
(August 22, 1991)

The coup attempt in the Soviet Union
failed.
Most Soviet Republics declared
independence.

The collective economy
dead.
Free market is the desire of the people
everywhere.

Freedom of speech, religion, choice,
And democratic government—
people want what is best
for them.

A free-market
world economy,
Where everyone can compete
and trade freely.

Nationalism

Are we moving to a state of
Nationalism?
Individual republics that want to
compete in the world economy?

Does each state and republic
want to become an owner state?
Does a state own
its natural resources?

Who owns America?
Who owns the Soviet Union?
Who owns China?
Who owns Canada?

Is it the central government
or each individual state?
Does not each republic have its own
agenda?
How does it relate to the whole?

Pacific Rim League

When will the world series
become a world series,
rather than American teams
playing with each other?

Maybe we need
a Pacific Rim League.
Anchorage, Tokyo, Beijing,
Hong Kong, and Khavhorisk,
playing for the world championship.

The world series
will become a true world series,
and the winner
will represent the best in the world.

Let us begin,
baseball fans of the world.
Cheer with beer
and bring us near.

Women of 2000

Awaken, women of 2000—
become the pilots, preachers,
pundits, and politicians
of tomorrow.

Assume the leadership,
take command,
assume the responsibility,
and all that goes with it.

As for me,
I say, "Go for it."

David Moe

Religious Revival

The Holy Spirit
is on the move
among people who are receptive
to the gifts.

Russia and China—
where the Spirit has been suppressed—
the Spirit is active
where it has been denied.

Revival is taking place
all over the world.
America will also awaken
when the Spirit is ready.

Independence

This is my declaration of independence
to the world.
I am no longer dependent
on the expectations of others.

I have found my freedom
through trust in Jesus Christ.
I have found new confidence
through His grace.

I am free
to write, sing, and serve.
I am free
to give my life to others.

I am free
to feel the joy and peace.
I am free
to be free.

Mind Pollution

What is the solution
to mind pollution?
Will it take a revolution
to reform this evolution?

Our youth are being bombarded
with music, pornography, and drugs.
Their souls are not highly regarded
by the pollutants of the mind.

So much art
is not enlightened,
but designed to dehumanize
and destroy the Spirit.

Let us unite
ecologists of the mind
to clean up the world
and the minds of all mankind.

Logic

Why do people who believe
in freedom of choice concerning abortion,
not believe in freedom of choice
for the education of their children?

Why do people who believe
in abortion,
not believe in capital punishment?

Why do people who believe
in capital punishment
not believe in abortion?

Why can't people be consistent?
Perhaps they are,
consistently inconsistent.

The Creation

In the beginning,
man created God
in His own image.
He created Him.

Man gave God
masculine attributes,
why not feminine
characteristics?

Man created God
with attitudes and emotions—
judgmental, cruel, destructive,
then kind, gentle, and loving.

The American Indian had it right—
the Great Spirit.

The Child

Within each of us
there is a child—
the child that was,
the child that is.

I speak to you now—
the child within—
the child that smiled
and played with a toy.

The child with imagination—
Superman, the Lone Ranger,
a bus driver, preacher, and politician,
all within a few minutes.

The child within
may be an abused child,
a lonely child,
but always a child.

Inner Peace

So much has been written
about peace in the world,
peace on earth, peace be with you,
shalom.

Peace is more
than the absence of war,
more than tolerance,
more than acceptance.

There can never be peace
between individuals or nations,
until there is peace within ourselves—
that inner peace that passes understanding.

Health Care Reform

There is much concern
about health care reform,
passing the risk
to someone else.

Health care reform is needed
to change our lifestyles
and attitude towards drugs,
to have freedom from pain.

Preventative health care
should be the emphasis—
proper diet, exercise, safe sex,
and moderation.

Care of the elderly and the young
should be our concern,
to lead lives free of fear
abuse and exploitation.

Rain

It is the rain
that made us all—
thin, short, fat, and tall.

All with which
and some with when—
smooth, tan, and then.

All with any
and much with some—
rest, sleep, and come.

All by night
and some by day—
who will ever, some may.

Thoughts will flow,
brain will fry—
all will pass by and by.

Cycle

Life is a cycle.
We go to foreign lands,
we fight on foreign sands,
but we return to our roots.

As a salmon
goes out to sea,
it will return to the river
where it was born, to spawn.

We go out
to experience the pleasures
of the world,
only to return.

God in the heavens
waits us out.
God knows we will return
from whence we came.

All of life
returns to the womb—
some call it death,
some call it the tomb.

Perseverance

The one who will succeed
in any walk of life
is not the strong, the wise, or the beautiful,
but those who persevere.

The one who outlasts the others,
the one who will not quit,
the one who accepts failure
as a stepping stone.

In business, sports, entertainment,
or you name it,
there are many who come and go,
but the one who stays the longest
is the one to reach the goal.

So don't give up,
don't be afraid to fail,
but learn from your failures
and persevere.

Things

All things sing
All things dance
All things live.

The breeze blows
Through the trees.
The seals slide
Through the seas.

The sea lions
Chase their pups.
The eagles watch
From the tree tops.

All things sing
All things dance
All things live.

Be Kind

Be kind to your family,
for they are the ones
who will love you all of your life.

Be kind to your friends,
for they are the ones
you can count on your fingers.

Be kind to the poor,
for they are the ones
who support and sustain your life.

Be kind to children,
for they are the ones
who will make your dreams come true.

Be kind to poets,
for they are the ones
who can give you immortality.

Time-Out

On Little Diomede Island
in 1993,
The people changed their time zone
for berry picking time to see.

They wanted their children,
to walk to school in daylight.
Subsistence hunters wanted to see
if they might.

They didn't want the federal government
telling them when to wake
and when to sleep.

Washington, D.C. officials
said, "No."
Time zones are imposed by Congress—
these people must be educated.

It is time
for a time-out.
Let common sense be the rule,
who is the fool?

Professional Pastors

A pastor is a shepherd,
One who cares for his flock.
One who loves, prays, and feeds,
Rather than entertain and shock.

Jesus said, "Feed my lambs,
Love my sheep,"
Not set yourself up
For others to keep.

Jesus was not a professional,
He had no degrees.
He had no confessional,
But He healed our disease.

Professional Pastors
Like Jim Baker and Jimmy Swaggart
Write books for money, as in
Pastors do more than lay people.

World Orchestra

We are the orchestra of the world,
each playing our part
with flute, viola, or harp . . .
music for our souls.

When we are in tune
with one another,
the music is beautiful . . .
there is no discord.

When we are in tune
with the Master,
the pitch, harmony, and rhythm
are united in one concerto grosso.

So let us get in tune
with the Master and one another,
so the world orchestra
will be in tune with the universe.

Dog Gone
June 30, 1987

It seems yesterday
we brought you home,
round little puppy
full of love.

Children were excited
wanting to hold
and pet
you.

Every day
you were here,
waiting to be
hugged.

Specific events (leg in a trap)
are fluid
in my memory
now.

Today,
I'll never forget
my Lucky Dog—
gone.

The Erl King

Goethe wrote the narrative ballad
of a father riding horseback
through a storm
with his sick child in his arms.

The delirious boy had visions
of the Erl King,
the legendary king of the elves
who symbolized death.

The boy cried out,
as did Jesus on the cross,
"My father, my father,"
when he faced the Erl King.

Shubert wrote a song
in 1815,
that ushered in a new age
of Romanticism.

The father arrived home
with his dead son in his arms,
thus ending
the Classical Age.

Healing

My father had an operation
at Mayo Clinic long ago,
the incision was left open
to let the poison flow.

When our inner self
is injured,
it must heal
from inside out.

All the anger, frustration,
and torturous sin
must ooze
to let healing begin.

So open the wounds
of your soul,
to let the stench out
and become whole.

Theology

A learned man asked
"What is your theology?"
I said, "Sir, I can
explain it in four lines."

Jesus loves me, this I know,
for the Bible tells me so;
little ones to him belong,
we are weak, but He is strong.

U.S. Navy Memorial

*The lone sailor
standing by his seabag
with his hands in his pea coat.*

The memorial reminds me
of the men I knew,
like Duffy, who won the Congressional Medal
in Korea,
but couldn't win against alcohol.

Young men
far from home,
lonely, confused, hungry too,
but will to serve
and die for you.

Control

Parents/children/
husbands/wives/
managers/employees/
unions/members/
preachers/congregations/
theologians/God/
directors/actors/
politicians/elections/
teachers/students/
students/time

The name of the game
is control—
it gives a sense of power
to the insecure
and frustration
to the rest of us.

The Body
(1 Corinthians 12:12)

The body has many parts
but is one body,
as the body of Christ—
though many is one.

The head looks at the body
but cannot feel
all the parts—
the nerves are paralyzed.

Christ, being the head,
looks at His body,
does not feel all of the parts—
members have withered.

Doctors of theology
diagnose each of the parts—
clergy, like nurses,
follow the doctors' opinions.

The head looks at
the parts—
why don't they work together,
for the good of the whole?

When will the body
function as a whole?
The head is waiting
for the body to respond.

There Are Looks

There are looks in the eyes of my mother,
> *when I ran outside naked.*
There are looks in the eyes of my father,
> *when I refused to do what I was told.*
There are looks in the eyes of my teacher,
> *when I had fallen out of a tree.*
There are looks in the eyes of a classmate,
> *when she learned her brother had gone down*
> > *at sea.*
There are looks in the eyes of my neighbor,
> *when he had heard a dirty story.*
There are looks in the eyes of my uncle,
> *when he had returned from the war.*
There are looks in the eyes of my aunt,
> *who didn't understand anymore.*
There are looks in the eyes of my grandfather,
> *when his farm had been taken away.*
There are looks in the eyes of my grandmother,
> *when there was no money to pay.*
There are looks in the eyes of a girlfriend,
> *when I broke an ankle in a football game.*
There are looks in the eyes of my coach,
> *when he knew I would not play again.*
There are looks in the eyes of an audience,
> *when we're singing praises to God.*
There are looks in the eyes of my voice coach,
> *when I told her I didn't care for opera.*
There are looks in the eyes of my English professor,
> *when I had asked her for a date.*
There are looks in the eyes of a coed,
> *when I showed up hours late.*

                    David Moe

There are looks in the eyes of my brother,
>   *when he told me he was going to marry my girl.*
There are looks in the eyes of my mother,
>   *when I told her I was going into the Navy.*
There are looks in the eyes of the chaplain,
>   *when he sent his daughter off for an abortion.*
There are looks in the eyes of a secretary,
>   *when she is totally ignored.*
There are looks in the eyes of a date,
>   *who had hot pants.*
There are looks in the eyes of my students,
>   *when I learned they could not read.*
There are looks in the eyes of another teacher,
>   *when I learned she liked young boys.*
There are looks in the eyes of my wife
>   *when I forgot her birthday.*
There are looks in the eyes of my daughter,
>   *a baby in my arms.*
There are looks in the eyes of a fellow seminary student
>   *when we were told the Holy Spirit doesn't call.*
There are looks in the eyes of the Vietnam vet,
>   *who gave his all.*
There are looks in the eyes of a widow,
>   *whose husband was shot for marching.*
There are looks in the eyes of my dog
>   *when I came home for the evening.*
There are looks in the eyes of Soviet children,
>   *I will not destroy your dreams.*
There are looks in the eyes of street people,
>   *no one really cares.*
There are looks in the eyes of politicians,
>   *who have just manipulated an election.*
There are looks in the eyes of people,
>   *skeptical and deceived.*

There are looks in the eyes of people
who don't know what to believe.
There are looks in the eyes of everyone,
looks of denial, not whole.
There are looks in the eyes of me,
for all these looks are a part of my soul.

God's Poems

We are God's poems
created to create,
to paint, to sing, to dance,
or to write.

We have been
created to create,
to make the world more beautiful,
not imitate.

Many people are depressed;
they need a new word
to lift their spirits
like a bird.

The Garden

The earth
is a garden—
the ocean,
pools.

We must care
for the garden—
tend the needs,
hoe the weeds.

We must share
the garden—
share the fruit,
preserve the beauty.

All are responsible
for the garden,
as Adam and Eve
in the beginning.

Family Reunion
1988

I attended a family reunion
in Minneapolis this past summer—
met cousins, aunts and uncles,
each march to a different drummer.

When I was in the Soviet Union
in October, 1986,
or Bangkok, Thailand,
in November, 1988

I met people who looked
like my relatives back there;
all had children
with loved ones who care.

We are one family, one people.
We need a family reunion
to reconcile our differences
with God and one another.

We need to keep our uniqueness,
yet be united in love,
to fight disease, depression, and destruction
and glorify the One above.

Heavenly Host

The great white multitude,
like snow-capped mountains
before the throne
of grace.

The hidden church
has finally come together
to rejoice and sing
praises to God.

Jesus, the shepherd,
stands radiant before them
as they look at the tree of life—
the cross.

This great spiritual body,
united at last
for all eternity,
forgiving the past.

For by His stripes
we are healed,
and by His blood,
we are saved.

The Restless Soul

When I was in the Navy
everything was go.
The old chief asked, "What is it
this time, Moe?"

I am never satisfied,
I want to try it all.
I want to write, act, sing and dance,
make money, teach, sell, explore,
and more.

The restless soul
is difficult to please . . .
My wife has stopped trying
to cure my disease.

One day my soul will rest
in some forgotten plot.
I will have done some
of what I thought I ought.

Prison

When I first visited prison
and heard the sound of the door,
I felt I would be there forever—
no more.

I continued to return
visiting one-to-one,
getting to know another human—
someone.

All of us are prisoners
of the patterns of our dreams.
All of us are isolated—
it seems.

Unlock the gates
of your mind,
let your feelings soar—
be free.

Maybe total freedom
is only a vision.
Most of us are more confined
outside of prison

Two Worlds

We live in two worlds
the world of the flesh,
the world of the spirit—
in conflict.

Satan controls the first,
Jesus Christ the second.
We are in the crossfire—
burning with desire.

Satan and his demons
attack us day and night,
we think we are strong—
but we are weak.

Put on the whole armour,
withstand the attacks.
Jesus is the only source
over evil and remorse.

Persons of Color

Some see the world
as black and white.
Americans seem to—
what color are you?

Some see the world
as red and yellow.
Orientals often do—
what color are you?

Some see the world
as pink and purple,
with rose colored glasses through—
what color are you?

Some see the world
as orange and green,
the Irish surely do—
what color are you?

Maybe everything
is a shade of gray,
color only a reflection—
of you.

The Office

Offices are unique—
colored phones, potted plants,
oak desks, computers,
nothing cheap.

Our office
is different than most—
low-key, old furniture,
burnt toast.

Office hours
are posted—
nothing clear,
but we're usually near.

Our office
is small—
no politics,
but fun for all.

Heartstrings

The strings of the lyre,
the strings of the harp,
are the voice
of God.

The strings of Jesse,
the psalms of David,
the songs of Solomon,
the voice of Jesus.

Strings bring music,
harmony, and healing
to my soul.

Do not play
my heartstrings,
unless you are serious
about music.

Poetry

When does a word
become a play?
When does a noun
become an object?

When does poetry
become a painting?
When does music
become a poem?

When does reality
become a fantasy?
When does a dream
become real?

When does the spirit
become flesh?
When does life
become eternal?

Eye of Alaska

The gulf of Alaska,
the eye of Alaska,
winking and watching
Prince William Sound.

The old blue eye
with white brows
and an icy stare
of care.

Then Exxon said,
"Here's oil
in your eye,
kid."

The old eye
only blinked . . .
It has seen its share
of folly.

Else

The Else family
has variety;
they perform many functions
in our society.

When there
is work to be done,
we call *Someone.*
Let Someone Else do it.

When we
are being accused,
we call *Anyone.*
Anyone Else could have done it.

When we
are being praised,
we call *Who.*
Who Else?

When we
are being questioned,
we call *What.*
What Else?

Pronouns

When things
are going well—
It is I.

When things
are going foul—
It is they.

When things
are uncertain—
It is we.

When things
are a disaster—
It is you.

When awards
are to be given—
It is I.

Repression

Silent and passive
we pass the day,
going through the motions—
let others pray.

We build barriers
without saying a word,
we are polite and smile—
we glide like a bird.

Inside
there is tension and stress,
anger is boiling—
emotions a mess.

Repressed emotions
are dangerous and corrupt,
they lie there boiling—
ready to erupt.

Eat My Words

The newspaper
is delivered by a teen.
I go to meet—
but I can't eat.

The newspaper
provides food for thought.
I read—
but I can't eat.

The newspaper
is filled with words.
I digest—
but I can't eat.

The newspaper
provides recipes and diets.
I'm discreet—
but I can't eat.

The newspaper
you can't beat.
I enjoy—
but I can't eat.

Rights

We have our rights—
civil rights, women's rights,
students' rights, workers' rights,
but who is right?

Who has the greater right?
A mother or a fetus?
An employer or a worker?
A husband or a wife?

Where will it end?
Human rights in foreign policy?
There is no end to the right
from the left.

What happened to responsibility?
Can there be rights without it?
Duty and responsibility
died with our rights.

Sports

To what extremes we resort
when we discuss our favorite sport,
for Americans are obsessed
with sports they like the best.

The French prefer undercover,
the Canadians out-of-doors,
the Irish, their favorite pub,
while Americans cheer for scores.

Think of the billions of dollars
spent each season,
getting a ball in a hole
for no apparent reason.

Sports are not for thinkers
or so it has been said,
for soccer is the only game
where one must use the head.

Humor

Humor
is a delicate art.
It must have balance—
not be smart.

Of humor that offends—
insulting, ethnic,
vulgar and political—
we should be critical.

We should be the protected—
not the target.
Humor insurance
should be on the market.

Whole laugh policies
should be for sale,
so we can file suit—
jokers to jail.

Humor insurance,
with lots of exclusions,
could be a joke—
like other conclusions.

Nostradamus

Nostradamus predicted
the famines of 1986—
the year of the comet—
the St. Francis earthquake
of 1989 (no need to
comment on it).

He also predicted the beginning
of World War III,
to begin in 1994—
the third Antichrist
to be an Arab with a blue turbin,
Christianity against Islam.

New York City to be
attacked,
twenty-seven years of war—
Arabs and Christians
Doing battle for the souls
of mankind.

Then there will be
a golden age of peace,
one thousand years of prosperity—
people living in harmony
until the world ends.

Silence

All poetry
moves
toward silence.

Seeds germinating,
fetuses growing,
tragedy, death—
all are silent.

The silent poets
are never heard,
yet their energy is as great
as the prolific.